Everyone in Invergarry village is talking about the Commonwealth Sports Day. Everyone is excited, especially Harriot McDougall.

3

That's because the Commonwealth Sports Day is a huge sporting event and Harriot loves sports.

Harriot plays throw and catch everyday with Fergus.

She often goes cycling through Glengarry Forest.

Harriot's friends also enjoy sports. Bonnie the
Shetland pony runs through buttercup fields.

Haggis the Highland cow jumps over fences and gates.

Harriot's family decide to go to the Commonwealth Sports Day. Harriot cannot wait! They drive in the McDougall Truck all the way from Invergarry village in the Highlands to Glasgow, where it is held.

The stadium is packed with people from all over the world. From South Africa to Barbados to India and Ireland too. They are all waving their flags to and fro and hoping the athletes from their country will win the best prize: the shiny gold medals.

But Harriot is bored sitting and cheering the athletes on. She has an idea, "Let's win the gold medals for Scotland!" she exclaims.

When the whistle goes for the 100 metre race Harriot sneaks out onto the pitch. Harriot runs faster than a cheetah for Scotland. Everyone is cheering.

When the whistle goes for the 200 metre swimming race, Haggis sneaks into the pool. Haggis swims faster than a sailfish for Scotland. Everyone is cheering.

When the whistle goes for Rhythmic Gymnastics, Bonnie gracefully jumps through a hoop. Bonnie jumps for Scotland. Everyone is cheering.

Fergus runs a lot and everyone cheers him on too.

Harriot, Haggis, Bonnie and Fergus are exhausted after competing in the Commonwealth Sports Day. They are glad to return to their seats in the audience.

Bonnie exclaims, *"Oh bother Buttercup!"* Haggis moos, *"Fluffety fluff, that was some tiring stuff!"* Fergus woofs to Harriot, *"Don't go getting yourself into any more trouble girlie!"*

There is an announcement. It is time to announce the winners. Harriot is nervous, but excited.

"3rd place for Rhythmic Gymnastics goes to Bonnie the Shetland pony, she takes home the bronze medal for Scotland!"
Bonnie neighs and everyone cheers.

"2nd place for the 200 metre swimming race goes to Haggis the Highland cow, he takes home the silver medal for Scotland!"
Haggis moos and everyone cheers.

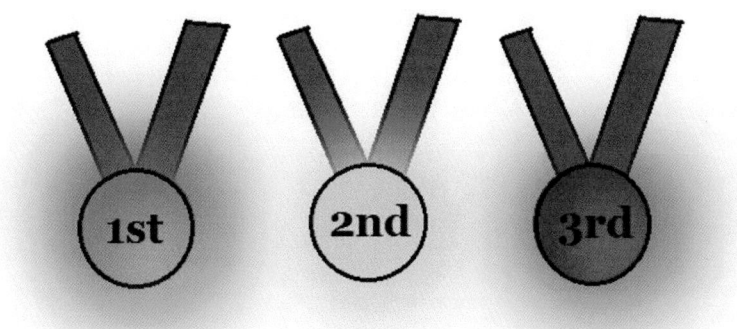

"1st place for the 100 metre race goes to Harriot McDougall and Fergus the Scottish Terrier, they take home gold medals for Scotland!"
Fergus woofs and everyone cheers.

"We have won the shiny gold medals for Scotland. *Yippee!*" Harriot cheers in delight.

Harriot whispers to Fergus, "See, you can be a winner if you try your very best." Fergus wags his tail.

For a wee lass from a small village up in the Highlands, being part of the Commonwealth Sports Day is fantastic.

"It's the taking part, not the winning, that's the best part!" says Harriot.

THE END

THANK YOU FOR DONATING TO CHILDREN'S CHARITY to Help Children Be the Best they Can Be!

Bonnie exclaims, *"Oh bother buttercup!"* Haggis moos, *"Fluffety fluff,"* and Fergus woofs, *"Don't go getting yourself into trouble girlie!"* as Harriot prepares for her next adventure!
See you soon.